Photo Credits: Cover and all photos by Maura Boruchow
Contributing Editor: Jennifer Silate
Book Design: Victoria Johnson

Visit Children's Press on the Internet at:
http://publishing.grolier.com

Library of Congress Cataloging-in-Publication Data

Foley, Cate.
  Let's go to the aquarium / by Cate Foley.
    p. cm. -- (Weekend fun)
    ISBN 0-516-23192-8 (lib. bdg.) -- ISBN 0-516-29582-9 (pbk.)
    1. Aquariums, Public--Juvenile literature. [1. Aquariums, Public.] I. Title. II. Series.

  QL78 .F59 2001
  597'.07'3--dc21

                                                                    2001017272

j J
Easy
Foley

Let's Go to the

Aquarium

By Cate Foley

Children's Press
A Division of Scholastic Inc.
New York / Toronto / London / Auckland / Sydney
Mexico City / New Delhi / Hong Kong
Danbury, Connecticut

Contents

We are going to
the **aquarium**.

Many different animals live
in the aquarium.

All of the animals live
in water.

.

7

The aquarium has many fish.

The fish live in **fish tanks**.

We see many kinds of fish in the aquarium.

Some fish are very little.

12

13

Some animals at the aquarium are very big.

This is a **killer whale**.

15

We also see **seals** at
the aquarium.

They like to play with balls.

17

There are also **dolphins** at the aquarium.

They really like to jump!

18

19

We had a fun day at the aquarium.

What did you like best?

New Words

aquarium (uh-**kwair**-ee-uhm) a building where water animals and plants are shown to the public

dolphins (**dahl**-fuhnz) sea animals with snouts that look like beaks

fish tanks (**fihsh tangks**) large containers that hold fish

killer whale (**kihl**-luhr **wayl**) a whale that kills and eats fish, seals, and even other whales

seals (**seelz**) sea animals with large flippers

To Find Out More

Books
Learning about Aquarium Fish
by Steven James Petruccio
Dover Publications

My Visit to the Aquarium
by Aliki
HarperCollins Juvenile Books

Web Site
New England Aquarium Kid's Space
http://neaq.org/learn/kidspace
Learn about sea life with fun projects on this Web site.

Index

About the Author
Cate Foley writes and edits books for children. She lives in New Jersey with her husband and son.

Reading Consultants
Kris Flynn, Coordinator, Small School District Literacy, The San Diego County Office of Education

Shelly Forys, Certified Reading Recovery Specialist, W.J. Zahnow Elementary School, Waterloo, IL

Sue McAdams, Former President of the North Texas Reading Council of the IRA, and Early Literacy Consultant, Dallas, TX